THE F.C.'S HANDBOOK

The FC's HANDBOOK

J.S.M. Ward

LEWIS MASONIC Books

Uniform with this book and by the same author

The EA's Handbook
The MM's Book

ISBN 0 85318 0806

Eighth impression
© 1988 LEWIS MASONIC
Terminal House, Shepperton, Surrey
Members of the IAN ALLAN GROUP

Printed by Ian Allan Printing Ltd

PREFACE

THOSE who have read the first volume of this series, which deals with the E.A. Degree, will realize that our ceremonies have a deep inner meaning and teach profound spiritual lessons seldom realised by the average Mason.

In the second volume we are dealing with the degree of Life, in its broadest sense, just as in the first degree we were dealing with the degree of birth, and as life in reality is educational for the Soul, we are not surprised to find that throughout the whole degree the subject of education is more or less stressed.

We should, however, realize that each of the degrees builds on the one which has gone before, and the ingenuity with which the lessons inculcated in the first degree are carried forward and developed in the succeeding degrees is one of the most striking characteristics of our Masonic ritual.

This is true not only of the obvious exoteric moral instruction conveyed in the ceremonies, but even more of the deep mystical and spiritual lessons which lie hidden beneath the surface. For example, in the first degree we perceived that the st....s which led the initiate to the Ped. when combined with that which we found thereon symbolically produced the Name of God, and in the second degree the main lesson is that the Brn. discover the name of God in the M. Ch., while the manner of approaching the Ped. gives us the Divine name, written with the five letters which denote that the Creator has become Messias, the King. Thus among other lessons we learn that the second person of the Trinity comes forth from the first. When we come to the book which deals with the M.M. we shall perceive that that degree likewise builds on what has gone before.

In the first few years of my Masonic career I utterly failed to realize the tremendous importance of the second degree, and used glibly to say that, while the first and third degrees impressed me greatly, and had valuable lessons to impart, the second disappointed me by its lack of depth and mystical teaching. Many brethren have said practically the same thing to me, but I have come to the conclusion that those of us who think this are mistaken. The truth is that the real inner teaching of the second degree is less obvious than that of the first and third, but every whit as important, and until one has grasped its full significance one has no conception of the wonderful symmetry of our Craft rituals. In short, the interpretation of the second degree forms the key to the full interpretation of the third.

It is to impress this fact on my Brn. that I have written this book, and in particular have laid so much stress on the manner of approaching the M.Ch., and the full Kabalistic meaning of the Name there discovered.

It must never be forgotten that while there are meanings within meanings in the Craft ritual, all of which are important, the great lesson of our system is the Mystic Quest after God, and the journey of the Soul towards union with its Creator.

With these brief words of introduction I venture to place in the hands of my Brn. this little volume, which, whilst not attempting to be exhaustive, will, I hope, be of some help to those who, amid the turmoil of mundane affairs, have little time to devote to an extensive study of the inner meaning of those ceremonies which they have nevertheless grown to love and venerate.

As one or two Brn. who have read this manuscript have asked me to refer them to a copy of the Kabala where they can themselves read what those ancient sages wrote concerning the descent of the letter " Shin," I would recommend the " Kabala Denuda," translated by Mathers, where they will find that, and many other points of peculiar interest to Masons.

J. S. M. WARD.

CONTENTS

Introduction by The Hon. Sir John Cockburn

INTRODUCTION

By The Hon. Sir John A. Cockburn

In this little volume W. Bro. Ward justly emphasises the importance of the 2°. In former times it was no mere passing stage of a Mason's career. In the Fellowship of the Craft lay the whole body of Masonry. An Apprentice was regarded as a brother but not as a member of the Lodge ; while a Master Mason was merely, as we still state in the ritual, an experienced Craftsman selected to preside over the Lodge in the capacity of Master.

The ceremony of Admission to the Fellowship of the Craft has been abbreviated and shorn of some of its characteristic features ; for example a " Mark," which, placed on the stones wrought by a Craftsman, entitled him to his wages, is now no longer allotted to him. Nevertheless it is in the 2° that the essential elements of the Craft are revealed. The degree is founded on that symbol which is the basis of Masonry, and is regarded as the test of rectangularity in the material, as well as of rectitude in the moral, world. The candidate is now enlightened as to the meaning of the " Hieroglyphic bright which none but craftsmen ever saw." He learns that it represents the ineffable names of the G.G. as written in the four letters of the Hebrew Alphabet, to which attention was specially directed in the M. Ch. . It is as a craftsman that he becomes cognisant of the second P.......r placed at the porchway of the Temple and he is taught that stability can only be attained by the significance of both P.......rs being conjoined. Herein is contained the Mystery not only of Masonry but of all the religions ; viz., the Union of Heaven and Earth and the Mediation between God and man. As an Apprentice he has been taught to walk uprightly in the sight of God : his mind has become imbued with moral principles : he now has to address himself to the much more difficult task of applying these principles in his everyday relationship with his fellows. The lesson of the J.W.'s plumb has now to be blended with that of the S.W.'s level. Spirit and Matter, theory and practice, with their innumerable analogies, have to be reconciled in solving the problems which are constantly encountered in life.

In the tables of the law one column contains the commandments relating to our duty to God, the other our duty to our fellow men. The Fatherhood of God involves as a corollary the Brotherhood of man. Therefore it is manifest that a stage in the progress of a Mason that lays stress on applied religion demands close attention. Although on the surface the ceremony of passing may appear less attractive than that which precedes and that which follows it, a close study will convince the reader that the 2° contains many lessons of priceless value which will well repay the labour of investigation.

J.A.C.

CHAPTER I

PREPARATION, P.W., AND OPENING CEREMONY

The questions which are put to the C. are really a test of the lectures, which to-day, unfortunately, are hardly ever given in open Lodge. The system as codified at the beginning of the 19th Century was really a most efficient method of educating the C., and had been carefully arranged so as to make sure that only when he was properly prepared should he come forward to be passed to the second degree. After having passed through the ceremony of initiation a summary of its main tenets, illustrated as it were on the blackboard, was given to him in the form of a lecture on the Tracing Board.

The Tracing Boards were originally drawn in sand on the floor of the L., and therefore correspond closely with the pictures and diagrams used among primitive savages in the initiatory rites of a boy into manhood. These primitive tracing boards are still drawn on the earth by means of specially prepared and consecrated flour, and are an essential part of the ceremony. To-day the masonic tracing board has degenerated into a somewhat crude painting on canvas stretched on a wooden frame, and its original purpose is therefore apt to be overlooked by the C. . This is peculiarly so in the case of the first degree tracing board, since the lecture on it is very seldom given. In the second degree, as will be shown later, the tracing board still plays a very important part, and we shall have occasion presently to consider it in full, but the connection of the tracing board with the questions must be grasped—hence this short preamble. Under the old system, at the next meeting of the L. the W.M. went through the lecture proper. He asked the S.W. a sort of catechism, which the latter had to answer. This would take well over an hour, or, in other words, as long as the ceremony of initiation. This catechism gave the exoteric meaning of most of the ceremony, together with a fair amount of traditional history of real interest. Undoubtedly much of it was allegorical, and although the bulk of it was 18th Century work, nevertheless it contained several very striking reminiscences of the Ancient Wisdom. For example, the question " Whence come you ? " A.—" From the W." .... Q.— " Whither directing your feet ? " . A.— " To the E. .... in search of a M." Here we have something of deep symbolical meaning, and of peculiar significance in view of a slightly different, though cognate, phrase in a later degree.

As, however, we are not attempting to interpret the meaning of these lectures in this book, we must pass the matter by, with the hope that our readers will make a point of obtaining a copy of them (purchasable at any Masonic furnishers) and study them at their leisure.

But the point which must be realised is that, while the tracing board is a summary of the first degree lecture, the questions asked of a C. are on that lecture itself. In short, the C. has to pass an oral examination, and the last question, namely, " These are the usual questions, I will put others, etc.," although to-day practically meaningless, had originally an excellent object. It indicated that the C., and also the other members of the L., had heard the full lecture and that the former must be prepared to answer any question on it.

In the North of England it is very usual, in addition to these questions, to ask the C. to repeat the whole of his O., and if he is unable to do so his passing is deferred until he can.

Turning to the questions themselves, it will be noticed that great stress is laid on the fact that the C. must be properly prepared. It is probably little known to most brethren, but well worth bearing in mind, that the Ancient Kabalists had a secret interpretation of the Old Testament, and one of the keys was to read backwards the Proper Names contained in those books. Now, if the words dedicated to the first and second degrees are read backwards, instead of the official interpretation given, they produce the phrase " Being fortified by the practice of every moral virtue, we are properly prepared." The significance of this in relation to what has gone before, and also to what will follow, is self-evident.

The inner meaning of the manner of preparation having been given in the E.A.'s Handbook, it is unnecessary to write further on the subject, but of course if any of our readers have not seen that book they should certainly get it, as otherwise they will fail to understand the importance of these early questions.

We now come to the question which is rightly termed a paradox. The explanation thereof, though ingenious, is obviously somewhat Jesuitical. The truth of the matter is that in Operative days lodges were held at mid-day, and probably on a Saturday, which has always been the time when the workmen receive their wages. The Speculatives, for their own convenience, changed the time to the evening, a fact which was resented by the old Operative members. In the first quarter of the 18th Century, at York, Operative Lodges continued to meet at mid-day, while the Speculatives met in the evening. To-day, with the disappearance of the Operatives, a Bro. may well wonder vhy this untrue statement is still left in the ritual.

The fact that it *is* there warns the careful student that some deep symbolical meaning must be attached to the time. The full significance of the phrase is only revealed towards the end of a Brother's symbolical career in the Craft, and a detailed discussion must therefore be postponed to another book, but it is permissible to point out the following facts :—The sun is at its full strength at Noon ; in his open pomp and glory ; vested, as it were, with his full regal powers. What more suitable time then for a solar cult to hold its meetings ? And we must remember that Freemasonry is distinctly solar in its symbolism. Again, we were told that the J.W. marks the Sun at its meridian, and we have seen that this officer represents the body, hence our meetings are held while the body is at its full strength, and in possession of all its faculties. Thus it is peculiarly significant that this question is put to the C. in the first degree, which degree deals with the " Natural " man. If the " Natural " man cannot protect himself at high noon against possible dangers, he is certainly helpless at any other hour of the day. We may therefore say that one meaning of this phrase is that the C. enters Freemasonry at the time of his greatest strength and physical well being. That this is not a fanciful interpretation is proved by the insistence that a C. must be perfect in all his parts. In the old days no man who was blind, maimed, halt, etc., could be made a Mason, and in Scotland a Master of a L. still has to take an Ob. not to admit such a man. The reasons for this are both practical and symbolical. As an Operative Society Masonry was like a modern benefit society and had to maintain sick Brn. and the widows of those who died. It is obvious, therefore, that they were justified in refusing to admit a man, not yet a Mason, who might easily become a burden to the society. Also, symbolically, every Mason is a sacrifice, and the Old Jewish regulations laid down explicitly that the ram offered for sacrifice must be without blemish, and perfect. These points must suffice for the moment, except that it is well to bear in mind that Christ was hung on the Cross at 12 noon, and our readers would be well advised to ponder over that fact and correlate it with Masonic tradition.

The next question and answer have misled many thoughtful Brn. as to the true meaning of Freemasonry. It should be remembered that it is addressed to an E.A., who as yet has had hardly any indication that Masonry is anything else than a system of morality. The first degree, for the most part, aims at teaching its members simply to be good men and true, and strictly to obey the moral law, but subsequent degrees teach much more than this. Until a man has grapsed these elementary lessons it is not only useless, but dangerous, to try to develop his intellectual facilities, which is the main exoteric purpose of the second degree. For a Mason who has taken his third degree to give this answer as an explanation of what Freemasonry is shows that he has failed to grasp the inner meaning of even the second degree, much less of the third. In short, this explanation by itself is only true when restricted to the first degree, for Freemasonry is much more than a mere system of morality, whilst even in the first degree the veil is very thin.

The Grand Principles, in modern language, may be interpreted as true comradeship, charity, and the search after truth, the latter phrase being better explained by the term the Mystic Quest after God.

The remaining questions are of a practical nature, except that the phrase P......t P.s. of my E. is often somewhat a mystery to the newly made Bro. . Two interpretations of this phrase are sometimes given. Firstly, that it refers to the S....p, which is a tau cross, and means that we will trample under foot our animal passions. This is the manner in which we enter the L. when once it is properly opened. But from the point of view of the C. it cannot refer to this, for at his initiation he did not know the S....p, and so the other interpretation is the only one possible, namely, " of, at and on." This is interpreted as meaning that the C. entered F.M. *of* his own f.w. and ac., *at* the door of the L., *on* the pt. of a S.I. . (See lecture). Having satisfactorily answered these questions the C. is led to the W.M., representing the Spirit or Wisdom, and receives from him a P.W., which will enable him to enter the L. when it has been raised to the higher degree. We have already in our first book explained briefly why P.W.s are necessary, but we will repeat our explanation for the convenience of any who have not yet read that book. They are a relic of old world magic. The C. goes out from a L. in the first degree and re-enters it in the second degree. In his absence the L. is raised by a ceremony which, in the technical language of magic and the occult, " raises the vibrations " of those present to a higher key, and in consequence force is generated. Those who have studied such matters know that a body of men who are all concentrating on a particular subject *do* generate a peculiar, subtle, but powerful force, which has not been actually defined by science but is loosely called magnetic. In the old days of phenomenal magic certain words, when uttered in the correct tone, were believed to be in consonance with this " Power," like a tuning fork is to a violin. Therefore we give a P.W. to the C. to raise him quickly to the same " Power," as the L. . Such P.W.s were usual in all great mystery rites, ancient or modern, and it is therefore not surprising to find them in Masonry. It is worth noting that the Ancients were right when they charged the so-called Moderns, in the 18th Century, with having altered the W.s and P.W.s. As a matter of fact they reversed them, and the W. now given to an E.A. was originally given to an F.C., and vice versa, and the same fate befell the P.W.s. Those foreign Gr. Lodges who derive from England before about 1745 (for example, the French and the Dutch), still have the W.s and P.W.s in the old order, and in

South Africa E.A.s and F.C.s of the Dutch Lodges are for this reason forbidden to visit the English Lodges until they have been made M.M.s.

The interpretation of this P.W. will be given at a later point in the book; all we need do now is to stress the fact that, as it is represented in our L. by C. and W., it is clearly associated with the J.W.. In the last book I pointed out that the J.W. represents in man, the body. This therefore indicates that to the spiritually minded man the simplest necessities of life are plenty. All he requires, as the Buddha taught, is sufficient to keep his body in health, whereas luxuries clog the soul and retard its upward progress.

I also pointed out in the last book that the J.W. represents God the Preserver, whose emblems in India, Mexico, etc., are C. and W.. From the anthropological point of view, it is worth remembering that among primitive peoples God the Preserver is also the God of Vegetation and the Rain God. He Who makes the corn to grow and provides food for his worshippers. Thus we perceive that Freemasonry is perfectly logical in its use of this W.. Another fact of interest is that Quetzacoatl, the Mexican Preserver, wears E.s. of C. in his hair when he is wounded by the giant of evil near to a

F. of W., and at that very instant makes the S. of a
F.C. .

The C. then departs to be prepared, and in the
interval the L. is raised to the second degree. We
will, however, consider the manner of his preparation before going on to the raising of the L. This
varies in several details. Most English workings
are the same, but the Scotch and Irish have certain variations which are worthy of mention. Ac-
cording to the Scotch rituals he brings into the
L. a sq. supported in his L.H., but, as with us,
the I.G. presents the angle of a S. to his N.B.,
although to the Rt. B. instead of to the L.B. In
the Irish Lodges the same B. is made b. as with
us, but he is still divested of all M.s as he was in
the first degree, and a C.T. is wound *twice* around
his neck. Thus it will be noted that everything
save the B. is reversed. The Scotch, more logical,
reverse even this. In American rituals the Irish
arrangement of the C.T. in the second degree is
also found. The reason for the deprivation of M's
in the Irish ritual is because, as with us, the P.W.s
have been reversed. This has a deep symbolical
meaning, and is logically correct, but I must defer
the explanation to the next book.

Reverting to the English method of preparation, we must realise that the R. side is the masculine side ; it is also the stronger side. It therefore implies, firstly, that we symbolically have passed out of the control of the women of the household and have gone on, as it were, to school. In the first degree we were symbolically " Babes " or children, under the care of women. In the second degree we are youths sent to be educated at school, and the whole exoteric meaning of the second degree is the training of the intelligence. This corresponds to a boy's training when he goes to a public school and is surrounded entirely by men. At home, under his mother's influence, he learnt only the simple lessons of morality ; the lessons of the first degree.

The second meaning, i.e. the stronger side, is stressed in the Scotch rituals, where the C. is afterwards told that he knelt on his r.k. to take his ob. because the F.C. ob.... is even more binding than the E.A.'s ob. This latter fact is also accentuated by the nature of the P., but this we will deal with later.

The C. is not H.......d, because clearly he is no longer in that state of absolute d...k.s which enshrouded him when he first entered Masonry. He has seen the L.......t, and can never again return to the same darkness, although he may not as yet fully understand all that the Lt. means, and it is to teach him the true nature of that Lt., which is really the Lt. of God, that he takes his second degree.

In view of what has been written concerning the preparation in the first degree, no further explanation is necessary.

THE OPENING OF THE SECOND DEGREE

The W.M. asks the J.W., representing the body, whether he is a F.C., to which the J.W. replies that he is, indicating the test to be applied. Now, what does the Sq. mean in this case ? It is not, be it noted, the W.M.'s square or tau cross, but it is an emblem of rectitude of conduct.

The right-angled square has always had this significance, and in many an Egyptian papyrus the Gods, when sitting in judgment on a soul, are depicted as seated on squares, implying that they are just judges. So the J.W.'s answer implies that he must be proved by his moral conduct in the physical world.

The F.C. degree indicates that the soul and body are now working in union, as is shown by the knocks, although, as yet, the purely spiritual faculties have little influence. So it naturally follows that in this stage of man's development we have a right to expect that he will conform to all the moral laws, and to the higher dictates of his nature. For example, he should have a kindly and charitable disposition. If he has these, he is a fellow craft, but as yet we must not look for great spiritual insight. It is through his body that a man is able to perform the moral duties of his station.

The S.W., or Soul, has little work to do at this stage, for it is through the body that we prove ourselves, and so it is the J.W. who is bidden to satisfy himself that all present are F.C.... This being done, he confirms their testimony in his own person, and the fact that he literally is proved on the square must not be overlooked.

It should be noted that it is no longer the Creative Aspect of God Whom we call on, but the Preservative. He Who places limitations on us for our preservation, for, unless we conform to the rules of the Great Geometrician we cannot hope to be preserved.

It should be remembered that by these ceremonies the Lodge has been raised to a higher plane of spirituality. Its spiritual and psychic vibrations are much higher, and to help the candidate to reach the same plane a P.W. has been given him.

CHAPTER II

PRELIMINARY STEPS

The Ty. gives the ks. of an E.A. for the Can., thereby emphasising the fact that it is an E.A., a stranger to a F.C. L., who seeks admission. The I.G. should therefore say, "There is an alarm," as *is* done in most old provincial workings, instead of "a report," a word suitable for announcing that there is a F.C. outside. Symbolically the difference between the ks. of an E.A. and an F.C. is most significant. The three separate ks. indicate that the body, soul and spirit are all equal and at variance, whereas the one and twopence show that the two lower, namely, soul and body, are now united. This means that the soul of the F.C. dominates the body, and in view of the fact that spiritual progress while on earth is dependent on this, the arrangement of the knocks is most important.

The C., having been properly announced, is admitted on the S., implying that he has been proved to be a man of rectitude and has therefore learnt thoroughly the lesson of the first degree, which is good morals. Throughout the whole of this degree stress is laid on the fact that only a man of good moral standing can be permitted to extend his researches into the intellectual spheres.

The other important point which is early impressed on the C. is the fact that God is called by a new title. He is no longer spoken of as the G.A., but as the G.G.. We shall revert to this point later, but even at this early stage it is desirable to point out that the aspect of God emphasised in the first degree was the creative aspect (Brahma of the Hindus), this is most appropriate for a degree dealing with birth, both physical and spiritual. The second degree deals with the preservative side of God ; it is essentially the degree of life, which is educational for the soul.

After invoking a blessing the C. is led round the L. with the sun and tested. Note, it is the body, or J.W., which now does the testing, but when the C. is led round the second time, to show that he is properly prepared and in possession of the P.W. which will make him in tune with the rest of those present, it is the S.W., or Soul, which tests him. Moreover, the Soul first satisfies itself that the Body has done its work properly, therefore the C. advances with S. and Sn., before giving the P.W.

Having satisfied himself on this point, the S.W.

calls on the Divine Spirit, represented by the W.M., for help, but as in the former degree, is told that it is the Soul that must instruct the C. to advance towards God. The Soul therefore tells the S.D., representing intelligence, to instruct the C. how to advance.

This method of advancing is exceedingly interesting, and worthy of detailed consideration. The F. Sp.s undoubtedly have reference to the five senses, which represent the physical man, whilst their spiral nature recalls the P. within a C. hinted at in the tracing board of the first degree, and reminds us that round it the Brn. cannot err. This clearly teaches us that we advance spiritually from within, by bringing under control all five senses and directing them towards that M.Ch. where dwells the Divine Spark, or God. As this subject will be treated at greater length when we come to the tracing board, we will merely point out that this manner of approach brings the C. to the V.S.L., which is God's revealed word. It should also be compared with the manner of approach in the first degree, which in the last book we saw disclosed the fact that the God we sought was within us, while His triple nature, and likewise that of man, is subtly suggested. Here we are taught the same idea, but from a slightly different angle, and are reminded that we are approaching Him by means of our five physical faculties. But as we arrive at the same place we perceive He is the same God, although during our ob. we learn of another aspect of His nature.

One other fact is worthy of our attention. Whereas in the first degree the C. was instructed to advance towards the P., in this he is told to advance to the E. . What is the reason for this difference ? It will be remembered that in the first degree he is H.W., and therefore unable to tell which is E. and which W. ; by the time he reaches the second degree not only can he see, but his previous experience tells him exactly where it is he will take his ob. . Esoterically, in the first degree he had no clear idea where to go for light, he was merely groping blindly, although led by a friendly hand : but in the second degree, having learnt that the true light comes from the E., there is no reason why this phrase should not be employed.

The position in which he takes his Ob. again makes the three S.s, but the instrument which he has to hold, and the manner in which he holds it, produce two more, making five in all — corresponding to the five senses, this irrespective of the

sixth on the A. or Ped. .   To begin with, these five
S.s indicate that all our senses must be dedicated to,
and ruled by, the strictest moral conduct, e.g.,
" Speak no evil, see no evil," etc., but when we recollect that in the first degree we got by means of
the Sq.s a suggestion of the Divine Name, we shall
not be surprised to find that here again the Divine
Name is indicated, but with two profound differ-
ences.   Firstly, the Name is complete within ourselves, that is, without needing to utilise the Sq.
on the Ped., and secondly, it is no longer the four
lettered Name of the Creator, Yod-He-Vau-He, but
the five lettered Name of the Preserver, Yod-He-
Shin-Vau-He, or *Yeheshuhe*, which we call *Jesue*
or *Jesus*.   As we learn from the Kabala, the Shin
has descended to earth and by combining with the
other four letters has made the Divine Name masculine instead of feminine, for *Shin* is masculine.
Secondly, it is the name of the Messiah.   Now it
has already been pointed out that the manner in
which the Can. K.s, and also his preparation, em-
phasise the masculine aspect of this degree.   Likewise the Name by which God is spoken of emphasises
His Preservative character, in contra-distinction to
the first degree where He is spoken of in His Creative
aspect and the feminine side is stressed.   Finally,

19

the fact that the whole Name is made by the man himself must be considered in conjunction with what has been said about the manner of advancing by the W.S....c., and the M.Ch. . The Kabala teaches us that Messias is made flesh, and this implies more than the fact that on a certain historic occasion God became manifest in a human body. It indicates rather that God is always being made manifest in every human being, and so the C., though he knows it not, is a manifestation of God on earth. Thus in a sense he himself represents the missing letter Shin, and so, when our ancient Brn. entered the M.Ch. to receive their wages and saw the mystic name Yod-He-Vau-He, they themselves represented that fifth letter, which turned the name of the Creator into the name of the Preserver and Saviour of mankind. Perhaps I should point out this is not strictly orthodox Christianity, but Kabalism, although its similarity to much that is taught to us as Christians is clear. Before leaving this subject I should like to remind any M.M.s who read this book of the manner in which they approach the Ped. in the next degree, for if correlated with what has gone before, the full significance of that manner of approach will be evident to them.

The Sq. on the Ped. indicates that there is still

another aspect of God about which as yet the Can. learns nothing, and its combination with the C.'s to make a lozenge should remind him that, though this degree is essentially masculine, God the Preserver has also His feminine aspect. The variation in the position of one of the points is explained at the time, but there is also a deeper meaning. One symbolical meaning of the Sq. is the material world, and therefore the body of man. In the first degree the body is dominant and over-shadows the spiritual side of the Cand.'s nature. In this degree the body is dominated by the soul, but as yet the spirit has not gained control over the latter. The C....m...ses, representing the higher or more spiritual side of man, reveal this fact by disclosing one point only.

The Ob. explains itself, and the Py. will be dealt with in the next chapter, as it can be more appropriately considered in conjunction with the Sn.s. As in the former degree, the Can. is r. with the proper g., which is subsequently explained to him.

CHAPTER III

THE S........TS

As before, the Cand. is taught by making the tau cross to trample under foot his animal passions, thereby reminding him that spiritual progress always entails increased moral rectitude. The first difference the Cand. notes is that the Sn. is of a three-fold nature. This no doubt has a reference to the triple nature of man, but to the Cand. the most important fact is that whereas in the first degree the Sn. refers only to the Pen., in this degree two other lessons are taught him. The first part is the Sn. of F., and implies not merely fidelity to his Ob., but obedience to the rules of the G.G.O.T.U. . We can only hope to be preserved if we conform to those rules laid down by Him for our preservation. The second part of the Sn., or H....g Sn., is said in our rituals to be the sign of P....y....r, or P....rs....e, but in its essence it is the sign of preservation, the sign associated with God the Preserver, under whatsoever name He is called, throughout the world. In my former book, " Freemasonry and the Ancient Gods," I have adduced abundant evidence of this and here it is only necessary briefly to summarise that evidence. In ancient Egypt it is associated with Horus ; in India with Hanuman, the skilful craftsman who built the bridge of Rama, the seventh incarnation of Vishnu, the Preserver. It was in this position that he brought the fruit of the tree of life to the dead and dying in the battle which Rama waged against Ravena, the Demon King. In Mexico, Quetzcoatl makes this sign when he is wounded by the evil giant. The Roman College of Architects at Pompeii painted it in a fresco depicting the preservation of Œdipus. The lineal descendants of the Roman Collegia, the Comacine Masons, in the 13th Century made a marble pulpit for the church of Ravello near Sorrento, not very far from the buried city of Pompeii. This pulpit they adorned with mosaics depicting Jonah coming up alive out of the whale's mouth and as he does so he makes this Sn.—H .. g Sn. and Sn. of F. complete. Now we are told that Jonah persevered in prayer for three days while he was in the belly of the whale, and was therefore preserved. Furthermore, we must recollect that the early Christians, their mediæval successors, and even the modern clergymen, have always regarded Jonah as the prototype of the Christ, for just as Jonah lay for three days in the belly of the whale and came forth alive, so Christ lay for three days in the tomb, and then rose from the dead. It is therefore not surprising to find that in England a 13th Century carving of the Holy Trinity at Peterborough depicts Christ making this Sn., for to us Christians Christ is the Preserver, since by His death we are saved. Thus it will be seen, firstly, that the Sn. is of great and genuine antiquity, and has been passed down by a regular line of successors from the days of the Ancient Mysteries ; and secondly, that it is clearly associated with God the Preserver and the idea of preservation. This fact emphatically shows that when we speak of the G.G.O.T.U. we are speaking of the Preservative aspect of God. It is also worth noting that except in London and those parts of England where the influence of London workings has spread, the l.a. is always held in a line with the shoulder, and not at right angles. In the ancient representations of it both the London and the Provincial forms are shown—a fact of considerable interest.

Among the various initiation rites of the savages, as, for example, among the Yaos, in Nyasaland, this Sn. is also used with the inner meaning of preservation, and two p.......rs form an integral part of their ceremonies.

The P......l Sn. is also old, for it is shown on numerous Egyptian frescoes and is referred to in the Book of the Dead. The significance of the Py. itself lies in the fact that among the ancient Egyptians the H...t was regarded as symbolising the good and bad in man. It was weighed at the judgment against the feather, the symbol of truth, and if a man's life had been evil the H...t and the Feather failed to balance and he was rejected. If therefore the H...t could not be produced, clearly the man was doomed to destruction. This point should be compared with the T...e in the first degree, and just as in that degree the Thr. was indicated because it is an important occult centre, so here the H...t is considered to have a similar significance.

The part pressed in the G. has always been regarded by palmists as masculine, just as in the previous degree it was feminine.

The meaning of the W. will be revealed in the chapter dealing with the tracing board, for obvious reasons, and those entitled to know will recognise where it occurs.

As before, the Cand. is instructed how to give and accept challenges and then is sent round the L. to be tested by the officers, who represent the Body and Soul respectively. This part of the procedure having been adequately dealt with in our first book, need not detain us now, for those parts which are peculiar to the second degree also arise in the tracing board. It is however worth noting that the phrase about the house standing firm for ever is not found in any passage of Scripture. It suggests the existence of an ancient masonic tradition, whose full history it is difficult to discover, but which is in closer analogy with certain phrases in the Book of the Dead associated with the Pillars, Tat and Tattu, which *do* convey the meaning thus indicated. It therefore looks as if we have here a genuine old tradition, now disguised under a Biblical form, but not derived direct from the Bible.

Once again the S.W., representing the Soul, calls on the Divine Spirit for some outward mark of his favour, and is told that he himself must invest with the distinguishing badge. To-day this badge has on it two rosettes, symbolising the rose, and made of light blue. Light blue was the colour of Isis, and later became the colour of the Virgin Mary. The Rose is her emblem, and these two facts imply that all below the M's. chair are regarded as passive or feminine, whereas only those who have actually ruled the Craft, and represented the Creative Spirit, are masculine. Thus on the P.M.'s apron we get the Tau Cross, instead of the rosette, an emblem of the masculine and creative power. The shape of our modern apron is undoubtedly of comparatively recent date. Our ancient Operative Brn. had large aprons, unadorned, and members of the different degrees were distinguished by the manner in which the apron was worn. Thus in the E.A. degree the triangular flap was worn with the point upward— the triangle of course represents the spiritual, while the Sq. part of the apron represents the material. It was worn up to indicate that the spiritual had not yet entered into control of the material man. It was usually turned down in the second degree, but, to distinguish between the second and third degrees, one or other of the corners was turned up. The apron was suspended by strings round the waist, and these are still used on the aprons of the first and second degree, although in a M.M.'s apron these strings have been replaced by a band of webbing. There are still aprons in the higher degrees however which are kept in place by cord and we shall consider the whole matter more fully when we come to discuss the M.M.'s apron, which is full of both historical and symbolical interest.

CHAPTER IV

CONCLUSION OF THE CEREMONY

When the S.W. has completed his task of investing the new F.C., the W.M. further points out that the purpose of the degree is to indicate that a Bro. must polish his mind by a study of the liberal arts and sciences. This reminds us that whereas the E.A. is likened to the rough ashlar, which rests on the J.W.'s ped., the F.C. is likened to the perfect ashlar of the S.W. . The two ashlars are respectively therefore associated with the J.W. as representing the body, and the S.W. as representing the soul. Thus once again we are reminded that although the E.A., as indicated by the knocks, has not yet subordinated the body to the Soul, the F.C. degree teaches the important lesson that the soul must dominate the body, and that the intellectual faculties must be educated so that the F.C. may the better discharge his duties to his fellow-men, and appreciate the wonderful works of the Almighty.

In the few operative lodges which still survive the indenture papers of the E.A. are, of course, torn up on his being made a F.C. . Another important

incident which takes place there is his formal testing to prove that he is a " square " man. This is
done by passing a four-sided square, the *four* arms
of which are extended, over his head and down to
his feet, whilst to see that he is *straight* a five foot
board, called the " straight edge," is placed against
the front of his body. The principal interest to us
speculatives of this peculiarly shaped square is that
by means of it half the secret masonic cypher was
produced. The rest of the cypher was made up
out of the St. Andrew's cross, used in the sixth
degree of the operatives.

After this brief admonition the Cand. is placed
at the S.E. corner of the L. and instructed to stand
in a position which forms a lewis, as in the former
degree. (See E.A.'s Handbook). Having explained
the reason for this, which symbolically denotes that
he is an adept, but not yet a master, the W.M. closes
his brief peroration with the peculiar phrase " That
as in the previous degree you made yourself acquainted with the principles of moral truth and
virtue, you are now *permitted* to extend your researches into the hidden mysteries of nature and
science." Now this is a very pregnant phrase and
often puzzles the Brn. . Only a few minutes before
the new F.C. is told by the W.M. that he is *expected*

to do this. Now he is told that he is *permitted* to do it. So puzzling is this to many Brn., that in one London ritual at least, the word *permitted* has been changed to the word *expected*. This change, however, in my opinion, is a grave mistake, for the word *permitted* is there for a very special reason. In the Ancient Mysteries it was believed that the masters of the higher grades held certain important secrets of nature, or, in plain English, had certain occult powers, such as second sight, hypnotism, and power to heal, and therefore, naturally, its reverse, the power to make men ill. To this day in India the higher Yogis claim the same powers. They claim also the power to communicate with beings not of this world. Now the ancient Masters of Wisdom declared that if these powers were obtained by a man of low moral character, on the one hand his very life might be endangered, by his attempting to get into touch with possibly hostile spiritual forces, while on the other, he might use these powers for evil, and so become a danger to the community. Therefore, only those who had given unmistakeable proof, through many years, that they were men of the most exalted moral character, were *permitted* to obtain that degree which entitled them to extend their researches into the hidden mysteries of occult science. Whether or not we to-day believe in such powers is a matter of personal opinion, although the hypnotic power is generally acknowledged by men of science. But, even if we restrict the meaning of the phrase to modern scientific knowledge, we shall perceive that there is here a most important lesson.

Every thinking man who has lived through the great war must realise that during it science has been used for the vilest, as well as for the best, purpose. Poison gas and the aeroplane which drops bombs on defenceless women and children are but two of many examples which makes us realise the dangers which threaten the human race if the hidden secrets of nature and science are discovered and used for evil purposes. Indeed, it is not too much to say that if we continue to make further scientific discoveries, and use them irrespective of our duties to our fellow men, we may utterly destroy civilization. Therefore this word " permitted " conveys a most profound message. It warns us that knowledge without morality may be a curse, and not a blessing. Thus we can see that the ancient Masters of Wisdom were wise in their generation when they refused to permit a man to delve into the hidden mysteries of nature and science until he had given proofs that his morality was such that he could be safely en-

31

trusted with those secrets. And so this little word *permitted* is one of the most important in the whole ceremony, and in no way conflicts with the earlier phrase that the Can. is *expected*. He is *expected* to study these secrets, and is told why : it is because he has made himself acquainted with the principles of moral truth and virtue in the former degree, and it is assumed that being acquainted with them, and having passed the tests which qualify him for admission into the second degree, he will in the future act up to these principles.

The explanation of the working tools is 18th century work, apparently, and requires no further explanation, whether we take the short form usually given in Emulation working, or the longer explanation sometimes given in some of the Lodges. Perhaps, however, the word *enthusiast* used in this connection needs a little explanation. It meant in the 18th century language, a " bigot " or an extremist, just as the words *zeal* and *zealot* did. In the course of years the exact meaning of many words in the English language alters, and some acquire a sinister meaning, while others become more kindly. To-day, the words " enthusiast " and " zealot " are generally used in commendation, whereas in the 18th century they were phrases of censure.

THE CHARGE

The charge after passing is not given in Emulation working, but as it occurs in some other workings it is deserving of a short mention. For the most part it is ordinary 18th century work, without any very deep meaning, but we may point out that a craftsman is told plainly that though he may offer his opinion on such subjects as are introduced into the lecture—i.e., the lecture of the second degree, now seldom given—he must only do so under the superintendence of an experienced master. In brief, he is not yet a fully qualified Freemason.

The other important point in the charge is the emphasis laid on the necessity for studying geometry. In operative days a sound knowledge of geometry was important in the laying out of the ground plans, and a careful study of the ground plans of Glastonbury, and other great mediæval churches, shows not only that geometry was of practical use, but that the main axial lines of the building were so drawn as to produce various geometrical figures of a symbolical nature. Many of these were of a most complex kind, and would require elaborate drawings to explain their meaning, we will therefore only mention the constant use of the equilateral triangle—the emblem of the Trinity—its duplication to form the lozenge, the circle, and the elipse, or the vesica piscis.

In general, Geometry symbolises the laws of the G.G.O.T.U., more especially those to be found in nature and science. Laws, be it remembered, which cannot be violated without jeopardising our moral and spiritual well-being, thus endangering our preservation, for which purpose they exist.

CHAPTER V

THE TRACING BOARD

The main teaching of the second degree is contained in the picture of the tracing board, and with regard to at any rate some of the incidents and facts an allegorical meaning is evident.

The first important architectural feature mentioned is a pair of columns, stated to have been set up at the porchway or entrance of the Temple. These pillars seem always to have had a peculiar fascination for our masonic ancestors, and even in the early days of the Comacines we find them setting up B. and J. in the porch of the mediæval church at Wurzburg, but their symbolical history runs back very much further even than the days of King Solomon's Temple. The two p......rs Tat and Tattu are found in the early papyri of the Book of the Dead in Egypt, and appear to have had the meaning of " in s." and " to e. firmly," but even in the primitive initiation rites of the Yaos, in Nyasaland, the boys, after various adventures, have to pass between two p.....rs. The original meaning of these p......rs was undoubtedly phallic, and in rites dealing with whence we come are obviously appropriate. The use of the word s. in a ceremony which, like these Yao rites, aims at increasing the procreative powers of the members of the tribe by a magical ritual, is obvious, but at a later date more ethical meanings were naturally grafted on to the basic one. That this original idea was not forgotten when the twin columns were set up by King Solomon is clear from the description of the chapiters. The net work, denoting union, combined with the lily work, denoting virginity, and the subsequent references to the pomegranates with their abundant seeds, convey the same lesson, as do certain other adornments of the columns, but already other more evolved ideas had been grafted on to the age-old symbols. Thus, the fact that they were formed hollow in order to serve as archives for Freemasonry, for therein were deposited, etc., seems to refer to the doctrine of re-incarnation. The constitutional rolls in this case are the effects of his past lives which are already latent in the child. At any rate it is clear that there must be an allegory here, for if intended to be accepted literally the statement is absurd. No sensible person would really put the constitutional rolls inside a hollow p........r, they would be placed in the muniments room of the Temple.

The reverence paid to p......rs or to monolithic stones is well known to every anthropologist, and undoubtedly was Phallic in origin. In the Bible, for example, we find constant denunciations by the prophets against the worship of stocks and stones ; the stock being a pillar of wood corresponding to the stone monolith, to which the worshippers were in the habit of addressing prayers containing the phrase " Thou hast begotten me."

The use of the two p......rs also reminds us of the gateway of birth through which we enter physical life, and so by analogy we get the idea that we must enter the mystical temple of Divine Life between similar p......rs. From such ideas would naturally evolve the suggestion that of the two p......rs one was black, the other white ; one of fire, the other of cloud. Thus we get the opposition between light and darkness, day and night, good and evil, male and female. Moreover, we do know that in many of the ancient mysteries, and in the savage initiation rites of a boy into manhood, it was very usual for the Cand. to be obliged to pass between two p......rs.

The opposition between light and darkness is also taught by the checkered pavement of our lodges. This pavement is a symbol used in many religions, and the Persian poet Omar Khayyam writes as follows :—

> " Life is a checker board of nights and days,
>   Where Destiny with men for pieces plays,
>   Hither and thither moves and mates and slays,
>   And one by one back in the closet lays."

Certainly this is one of the meanings of the mosaic pavement, although in addition, as Sir John Cockburn has pointed out, the word " mosaic " may be connected with the same root as the word Moses, which means, " Saved from the flood." If this be so, the checkered pavement would be derived from the mosaic effect produced by the receding flood of the Nile as it left the land on either side dry after the floods. Let us now consider the names given to these two p..... rs by the Jews. If we turn to the Hebrew words themselves we shall find that they had a secret inner meaning among the Kabalists. These Jewish sages had a special and secret interpretation of the Old Testament, and one part of this secret was to read certain significant names backwards. If this be done in the case of the two words under consideration we find that their conjoint and full signification is, *Being fortified* by the practice of every moral virtue we are now *properly prepared* to undergo that last and greatest trial.

The official interpretation given is not without significance as far as the first word is concerned, for God said that He would establish the House of David for ever, but while we can perceive the importance of the ancestor of K.S. what of the Assistant H.P.? Firstly, it must be recognised that the first column was considered to be the Royal column and the other the Priestly, and the explanation may refer to this. In that case we obtain a declaration as to the necessity for Church and State as the foundation for civilization. It is interesting, however, to note that those who look for a Christian interpretation of our rituals are able to point out that while the first name refers to the founder of the House of Jesse, the other name is that of the last male ancestor of Christ, namely the husband of St. Anne and the Father of the Virgin Mary. Thus the names of these two p.......rs represent the beginning and the end of the House of Jesse, from whom was drawn the body of the Saviour of Mankind.

As there is a school of symbologists who consider that the whole of the Craft degrees can be interpreted in the Christian sense, these facts cannot be ignored. If their interpretation is correct the apparently casual reference to H.A.B., the son of a W., takes on a new significance in association with these p......rs. In any case, in his progress through masonry this is the first mention that the Cand. hears of the famous Architect. H.A.B. is regarded as a prototype of the Great Master, and there does certainly seem to be a striking similarity between the chief incidents in the lives of both of them. But this fact will become more evident when the F.C. has taken his M.M. degree. :

Before leaving the subject of these two p....rs it is of interest to point out that p......rs are regarded as emblems of stability among many races, and on a " *chop*," or certificate, used by one of the great Chinese secret societies the character KEH, meaning a p......r, is used, which among them has the further meaning of Stability.

Sir John Cockburn recently pointed to a most pregnant fact. It is well-known that in the course of oral transmission foreign words become so corrupt in form that there comes a time when they cease to be intelligible, and in consequence attempts are made to replace them by a word whose meaning is known, and whose shape is similar to that of the corrupt word. Many masonic students suspect that this has occurred in our ceremonies, and Sir John suggested that the Greek words *Iacchus* and *Boue* were the original names attached to these p.......rs. *Iacchus* or *Bacchus* was the God of Youth and of the procreative powers, Who in some of the Grecian Mysteries was slain and rose again, while *Boue* means the primeval chaos, the dark womb of time, and so the womb.

This interpretation cannot be rejected lightly. Firstly, the appropriateness of such words to these two degrees is self-evident, but even more striking is the fact that the Supreme Council 33° of France gives to its members an esoteric interpretation of all the important words used in Freemasonry, and it interprets J. as the phallus, and B. as the womb. Spiritually interpreted this would mean that the God of Life and Light, Iacchus, descended into the womb of chaos and brought forth Life.

The tracing board having at considerable length, and in great detail, described these p.......rs, goes on to give a certain amount of information about the men who actually built the Temple, and a very clear distinction is drawn between the reward received for their labours by E.A.s and that received by F.C.'s. The E.A.'s, representing those who as yet are not very spiritually evolved, obtained merely simple maintenance, whereas it is specifically stated that the F.C.'s were paid their wages in specie, which, however, they could only receive in the Mid.

Ch. . In other words, their wages were of a spiritual nature, suitable to their more evolved spirituality, and that this was so is proved by the fact that they received them in the Mid. Ch., which is an allegory for the secret chamber of the Heart, where dwells the Divine Spark. In all mystical language, and all descriptions of mystical experience, this hidden chamber of the Heart is spoken of as the place where dwells God in man. It is in reality a state of mystical experience, where the soul realizes, and for a brief moment of time becomes one with, the Divine Source of all. That this is so intended is clearly indicated by the statement that when our ancient Brn. entered the Md. Ch. their attention was peculiarly directed to certain Hebrew characters, usually depicted in our Lodges by the letter G., denoting God, the G.G.O.T.U. . Now the Hebrew characters stood for Yod- He- Vau- He, or Jehovah, the G.A.O.T.U., but since, as has already been explained, each F.C. in himself stands for *Shin*, in combination with himself he finds in the Mid. Ch. the name of the Messiah, *Yeheshue*, (Jesus) Who is the G.G.O.T.U., or God made Flesh, Who dwells among us. Bearing this fact in mind we shall the better understand the ceremony of closing, wherein the J.W., representing the Body, declares that in this degree they have discovered a S.S., representing God. The fact that it is the J.W. who makes **this** announcement, and not the S.W., is explained by the correct interpretation of the W.St...c...se. This St...c...se is our own body, as we shall explain later.

The ancient Brn. were not permitted to ascend this St...c...se until they had satisfied the J.W. that they were truly F.C.s, but he did not ask of them the F.C.'s W. as one might expect, but the P.W. leading to that degree. This is of course right, for he deals with the simple necessities of life, which the E.A. receives, and which to the truly spiritual man, such as the F.C. claims to be, are plenty, whereas the true W., with its priestly meaning, belongs to the S.W. or Soul. The J.W. has no part or lot in that, but it is his task to see that the Body is in good condition, for a diseased body may easily hamper the Soul in its progress. Masonry deprecates those foolish ascetics who torture and ill-treat the body, as much as it does gross and luxurious livers, who over indulge the physical and thus hinder the soul's advance.

The explanation of the origin of the W., although taken from the Bible, no doubt has an inner meaning. In one version we are told that Jephtha, like

Joseph, and before him Ishmael, was rejected by his relations and went out from his father's house to a strange country. When, however, Gilead was threatened by the Ammonites and sent a deputation to him begging him to come to their help and organise armed resistance, he forgave the unkindness he had suffered and saved his native city. Thus we can see that, like One who came after him, he was " The stone which the Builders rejected," which became the headstone of the corner. So here again we get a reference to the Saviour of men and to Preservation.

The W. St....c...se with its three, five, seven or more steps, must have puzzled many thoughtful Brn., who have no doubt wondered why it was that those who codified our rituals could not make up their minds concerning the exact number of steps the St....c...se had. This very fact warns us that it is an allegory, for the thing disguised under this name can be considered to consist of three parts, five parts, seven parts, and possibly more. The three who rule a Lodge represent the Body, Soul, and Spirit which constitute Man. The five who form a Lodge are the five senses of the physical man. But the physical man has both soul and spirit, each of which has its own peculiar sense, the Soul having psychic faculties, and the Spirit mystical and inspirational. As the Bible indicates in the past there have been men who had second sight, and prophets who spoke by Divine inspiration. Although while on earth the ordinary man only functions through the five physical senses, those who are approaching perfection, such as the great Masters and religious teachers of the world, function through all seven. The reference to the five noble orders of architecture is certainly an 18th century addition, for our mediæval Brn. cared nothing about them, while the reference to the seven liberal arts and sciences is probably a post-reformation gloss. They are good enough for an exoteric interpretation, but obviously disguise something more profound. The five noble orders of architecture when applied to the Temple of K.S., are, of course, an absurd anachronism. Perhaps at this point one should explain that the Temple at Jerusalem, masonically, is an allegory for the Temple of Humanity raised to the glory of God, or, to use a Christian simile, the Church of Christ earth, into whose fabric every true mason is built, dedicating his body and soul as a perfect ashlar in its construction. This W. St....c...se spiralled round a central column, so that when the Brn. reached the top they had advanced neither to the East nor to the West, but were still revolving around the centre. To an Eastern Bro. this W. St...c...se will certainly recall the ladder of re-incarnation, by the gradual ascent of which the Soul in time returns to God, from Whom it came, travelling upwards in a spiral.

But to the Western mind this St....c...se is our own body, subdued, brought under control, and dedicated to the glory of God. This done we receive our wages, which are knowledge of God in that hidden chamber which is within us. No other man and no external organisation can really give us *knowledge* of God, that is an experience which each must discover for himself, and in himself, as every mystic has taught, no matter to what external religion he conformed. Mysticism is not an organised religion, in rivalry with any of the established faiths, but is the real truth enshrined in every religion, and the force which gives that religion vitality.

Therefore it is that we find among Mahomedans, Buddhists, Jews, Hindus and Christians, men who while they often employ different symbols, use them to describe precisely the same spiritual experiences.

Finally, let us note that the last guardian who has to be passed is the Soul, which itself passes the man who is a true F.C. into that hidden Ch. . When he has thus proved himself a true priest in the spiritual sense, the Soul enables him to discover the God Who is within him, and that this Divine Spark is ever linked to the Source of All. It should be clearly understood, however, that this discovery of God within ourselves is not the end of the Mystic Quest, for the evolving Soul has other experiences to go through, some of a most painful spiritual nature, before he achieves final and complete union with the Source of his being. But until he has had this first experience, this first realisation of the Divine Spark within him, he cannot start on the real quest ; for he is not yet properly prepared. He may, and will, come out from that secret Ch. again and again, to take his part in the ordinary life of the world, but having once glimpsed the splendour of the Divine he will realise the glorious heritage to which he is the heir and will not be content until he has completed his journey. Nevertheless, it may truly be said that these occasional experiences, brief and passing though they be, are the just reward of his labours. This then is the great lesson of the second degree, that by ourselves, and in ourselves, we can discover and realize God, more especially in His Preservative aspect. This discovery means more than an acquiescence in the statement of others that there is such a Being as God, it is the realisation by oneself of this stupendous fact, a thing almost impossible to describe in words except to those who have experienced it, while to them it needs no description.

CHAPTER VI

CLOSING CEREMONY

As in the first degree, the Spirit calls on the Body and Soul to show that they are on guard against this world. The Spirit then asks the body what it has discovered now that it has conformed to the laws of rectitude, as a true F.C., and the Body replies that it has discovered a S.......d S.......l. This S.......d S.......l, of course, is that same letter G mentioned in the tracing board, which corresponds with the Hebrew characters for the Name of God. As we have already explained the full significance of these four letters we will not now discuss them further, but a few brief lines dealing with the valuable suggestion of Sir John Cockburn, that the letter G was originally depicted in the mediæval lodges by a sq., calls for some consideration. Sir John has pointed out on many occasions that the sq., more particularly the gallows sq., was always regarded with very great veneration by the Masons, because not only was it an important working tool, with a symbolical meaning attached to it, but it was also the shape of the gamma, or G., in the Greek alphabet, as well as in the ecclesiastical script used in mediæval Europe. Thus the letter G and the gallows sq. were the same shape, and stood alike for God and His great characteristic, " Justice." Indeed, in mediæval paintings the sq. is often found embroidered on the vestments of the disciples, and when depicted separately these are called " gammadias," that is " gammas," but when combined to form the Swastica it is called the " gammadion." As Sir John points out, references to this identification of the sq. and the G. are found in several old rituals. For example :—

Q.—Why did you get to be made an F.C. ?

A.—On account of the letter G.—

Also an old masonic legend found in one of these rituals, describing a murderous assault made on one of the chief overseers of the work by some of the workmen, relates that one of the wretches struck the overseer a blow over the heart with a sq. . When the victim was subsequently discovered those who found him noticed a faint trace of the letter G on his breast, and they understood it as symbolising the whole-hearted devotion which the victim had always displayed towards God, the G.G.O.T.U.

Another interesting point about the sq. is that if four right angles are joined together with the angles inward, an equal-armed cross, or cross of the cardinal points, is formed. This cross, of course, has many inner meanings, but one at least is that it represents the earth and matter, just as does the four-sided sq., which also can be formed out of four gallows sq...s. Finally the Swastica, which later symbolised the sun, is also composed of four right angles; hence the vital fluid permeating matter makes of it a living soul. In this last aspect the Swastica becomes an emblem for God Himself, and thus the sq. in itself represents not only God, but also the universe, which He preserves by His Divine Spirit.

So it will be seen that the S...d S...l which the F.C.'s declare that they have discovered is of far greater significance than most brn. would suspect; in fact, in these few brief words of the closing ceremony we obtain a summary of the whole purpose of the degree, and realise why, throughout the whole of it, the sq. is emphasised. Nor must we forget that when he announces this discovery the J.W. stands in the correct position to indicate that he represents that fifth letter, the missing " sh," which changes the name of the Creator into that of the Preserver—Yeheshue. Moreover, he declares the S...d S...l is situated in the C...e of the build-

51

ing. Bearing in mind that in the tracing board we were told that our ancient brn. discovered this symbol in the M...e Ch., we shall perceive that the Lodge itself is now the Ch., into which the Cand. has ascended by the W...g S...c...e of the f... St...s which led him to the E.

The fact that it is in the C...e reminds us of that hidden centre in every man, where resides the Divine Spark, and brings to our recollection the statement in the first tracing board that there is a point within a circle around which the Brn. cannot err.

In lodges in the Provinces which have their own Temples, it is usual to see depicted on the roof a pentacle, in the middle of which can be seen the letter G. In this case the pentacle represents man with his five senses, with the G at the cente to remind us of the Divine Spark within. On the floor directly underneath is inlaid in brass a point within a circle, which circle is bounded on the north and south sides by two grand parallel lines, usually described as the two St. Johns, but stated in our ritual to represent Moses and K.S. . They also undoubtedly symbolize many other things, e.g., the two pillars of night and day, good and evil, male and female, etc. The point I wish to stress, however, is that the brass point at the c. of the c. is directly underneath the G in the pentacle on the roof, thus emphasising the interpretation we have been studying. It is a thousand pities that in most of our London Lodges both these essential ornaments of the Lodge are omitted from the decorations, as by so doing their intimate connection is apt to be overlooked by the brn., and even the words of the ritual become untrue. Thus the F.C. degree teaches us that we only begin to recognize the God within us when we have lived a good life. There is also, probably, a reference to the word " Generation," which is naturally associated with the life of the fully developed man. The meaning of this is that the power of begetting is a Godlike gift, for it creates physical life, and we must use it with respect and for the noblest ends. It is only when we are masters of our passions in this respect that we are fitted for the last and greatest trial.

It is noteworthy that it is the J.W., representing the Body, who plays the most important part in the closing of this degree, which is, of course, appropriate, as we have been dealing throughout with the body and its five senses. This phase is carried through to the very end, as is shown in the curious doggerel lines with which the J.W. performs the last act of closing. As given in Emulation they are only three, but in the Provinces they are four, and form a curious jingling rhyme, which runs as follows :—

> Happy have we met,
>   Happy have we been,
> Happy may we part,
>   And happy meet again.

Personally I prefer this version to that in Emulation which, for some unaccountable reason, omits the second line, although it is quite as important as the first or third.   Clearly the Brn. might be happy to part because they had been unhappy during the ceremony !   The inner significance of the lines, however, is that the body bears testimony that earthly happiness can only be found by those who know God.

The closing prayer by the W.M. contains one important reference, which seems to be an ancient landmark carried down in our ritual from a long distant past, viz., the All-seeing Eye.   This Sacred Eye was a divine emblem and an important talisman among the ancient Egyptians, even as it still is among the Chinese, who paint it on the bows of their ships to protect them and preserve them from misfortune.   It is essentially an emblem of God the Preserver, and its inclusion in the closing prayer of the second degree indicates how carefully the preservative aspect of God is stressed, from the beginning to the very end of the ceremony.

This concludes all that it is possible to deal with in this little book concerning the second degree, but those whose interest has been aroused will be well advised to do two things ; firstly to study the ritual itself, in order to discover additional inner meanings, which do exist, although they have not been dealt with here lest we should befog our newly passed Brn. ; and secondly, study the lectures on this degree, which contain a great deal of interesting information, much of it with an inner meaning seldom appreciated by those who have only read them through hastily. Finally we would add that in the M.M.'s Handbook will be found an explanation of several points which we have had to omit in this book, but which show how carefully each of our degrees is linked up with the one that follows, and how to the attentive student they gradually unfold many important and illuminating truths.